T0128660

Lily Tova
The Therapy Dog

Cynthia R Zeldin

Copyright © 2021 Cynthia R Zeldin.

All rights reserved. No part of this book may be used or reproduced by any means, graphic, electronic, or mechanical, including photocopying, recording, taping or by any information storage retrieval system without the written permission of the author except in the case of brief quotations embodied in critical articles and reviews.

Archway Publishing books may be ordered through booksellers or by contacting:

Archway Publishing
1663 Liberty Drive
Bloomington, IN 47403
www.archwaypublishing.com
844-669-3957

Because of the dynamic nature of the Internet, any web addresses or links contained in this book may have changed since publication and may no longer be valid. The views expressed in this work are solely those of the author and do not necessarily reflect the views of the publisher, and the publisher hereby disclaims any responsibility for them.

ISBN: 978-1-6657-1106-7 (sc)
ISBN: 978-1-6657-1107-4 (hc)
ISBN: 978-1-6657-1108-1 (e)

Print information available on the last page.

Archway Publishing rev. date: 09/24/2021

Dedication

This book is dedicated to my mom, Sophie Rutstein, who taught me what volunteering is all about. When I was a child, we would visit nursing homes and my mom would play the piano and I would sing to the residents. She demonstrated by example how to be kind and loving. I learned about justice, healing the world, charity and kindness to others. I will be forever grateful for having learned those lessons in life.

Much gratitude and love to Todd Zeldin for his love, support and encouragement throughout the entire process.

I would like to thank Steve Rabb for his expertise in marketing and development in helping me get through the final stages of this process.

Thanks to Barbara and Hank Kimmel for their love and friendship.

Thanks to John Davis for being there when I needed him.

Thanks to Alyssa Cerchiai for her help in finding the right words when I could not find them.

Thanks to Archway Publishing for their patience and support.

Most of all, thanks to Lily Tova, for teaching me what life is all about. She gives her love unconditionally and her generous spirit is never ending.

Lily Tova is a therapy dog. She visits people who are sick and in hospitals and she also visits schools.

She is a Havanese, and that breed is originally from Havana, Cuba.

Lily Tova's great, great, grandmother lived in Cuba.

After a while this breed came to America and is now one of the top breeds in this country.

Lily Tova is a very special dog who has been taught how to make everyone happy.

She had to meet hundreds of people. Tall people, short people, people with glasses, people in wheel chairs, small children, big children and even babies.

She had to pass many tests before she could become a therapy dog. This was very difficult for her but she passed with honors. She was a little over a year old when she started working and she has been a therapy dog for eight years and has over 300 volunteer hours.

Lily Tova visits schools where children read to her. She loves to listen to the stories and sometimes she tries to turn the pages.

One time she actually ate the pages of a book and that was very funny.

She is trained to know when someone is sad or needs special attention.

If she senses that you are sad, she will hop up on your lap and lick your face.

When she visits nursing homes she lets everyone pet her and she does all sorts of tricks.

One time she actually saved someone's life that had trouble breathing. She went near a lady who was in a wheelchair and just kept barking. Finally, I realized that Lily Tova was telling me that something was wrong. A nurse came very quickly to help the lady. Lily Tova was a hero because without her barking no one would have known the lady needed help.

Sometimes Lily Tova has to be just a plain mischievous dog. On her last birthday I put a cupcake on the table and she jumped on the chair knowing it was for her. I told her to wait until I got a candle and I gave her instructions to not eat the cupcake. BUT, when I went back into the room, there was icing all over her face and she looked very guilty.

Since it was her birthday I decided to let her have the whole cupcake and what a mess that was.

Lily Tova is so smart I decided to teach her another language.

One day I said "Lily Tova, siéntate". She turned her head to the side a few times and then I kept repeating it and pointed to the ground. Guess what? She finally sat down.

Oh my goodness I thought, what if I just give her all of her commands in Spanish?

So then I taught her baila, which means dance in Spanish.

Oh my, she loves when I play the piano and she just dances non-stop on two feet.

Baila (Dance)   Siéntate (Sit)

One time there was a very sick lady in a nursing home who only spoke Spanish. Sadly, there was no one there that could talk to her.

The lady was so excited to meet a dog that could understand Spanish, she said, "Lily Tova es mi corazon" which means Lily Tova is my heart.

Since Lily Tova is so smart, I decided to teach her to read. People have said that this would be impossible. She now reads ten words and is still learning new words every day.

Lily Tova does lots of tricks like sitting on her tush, begging for a treat and rolling over.

When I ask her if she wants to play a game, she gets all excited and jumps up and down. I then hide a treat in my jacket and she loves searching for it.

When she finds it, she hides the treat somewhere and then I have to go find it.

Lily Tova loves to play hide and seek.

One day, she hid in the garage. Another time she hid in my suitcase under a pile of clothes and all I could see was her nose sticking out.

She put her paws over her face because she knew she was being mischievous.

Sometimes when I am ready to take her for a walk, she runs all over the house, racing around the coffee table and then runs up and down on the sofa and finally stops, waiting for me to put on the leash.

Therapy dogs can also be a lot of fun even though they spend their lives helping others.

14

One day in February of 2020 a terrible thing happened all over the world, called covid.

People were getting sick and were in hospitals, and children were not allowed to go to school. Mommies and daddies had to stay home to teach their children.

Lily Tova, the wonderful therapy dog that she is, was not allowed to visit schools or nursing homes anymore.

People in the nursing homes were very sad. They could not cuddle Lily Tova anymore and missed her very much.

Covid was very bad and if people came in contact with it, they got very sick.

Covid spread germs all over the cities and towns.

No one could go to school anymore. No one could go to the park or visit their friends.

It was a very sad time for everyone.

All the stores closed, all the restaurants closed. All the people who used to go to work every day stopped going and now everyone had to stay home.

Daddies and mommies who used to go to work were now told to stay home.

Children could not have play dates anymore. The only thing you could do was go for a walk outside and you were definitely not allowed to be near other people.

It was a sad, sad time in this country.

Covid was everywhere. People were so scared of Covid, that they started to wear masks. Even doggies wore masks to keep Covid germs far away from them.

Lily Tova and I decided to visit the schools and nursing homes by using the computer.

Lily Tova and I were able to read stories to the children even though we could not be with them in person.

Lily Tova would put her head real close to the screen so she would feel like she was actually kissing her friends.

The children read her stories and we all sang songs together. Lily Tova was still being a therapy dog only she could not be there in person.

After many, many months, the smart doctors found a vaccine that could prevent people from getting sick.

It meant that everyone had to have an injection. Once they had the injection, they could be safe from Covid. Covid would now be gone forever.

Lily Tova was back at work letting all the children read to her. She was once again able to eat the pages of the books, and play hide and seek, and make everyone smile again.

Now children could go back to playgrounds and parks. They could attend school and go to camp. They could play with each other. Mommies and daddies could work again and things were happy once again.

Lily Tova, the therapy dog, was happy to be making children in schools and people in nursing homes happy and smiling once again.

She loved working and most of all she loved it when everyone surrounded her with love and lots of kisses.

Printed in the United States
by Baker & Taylor Publisher Services